A Treasury of

Christmas Humor

Monsters Unchained!
More Anguished English
The Play of Words
Presidential Trivia
Pun & Games
The Revenge of Anguished English
Rip Roaring Animal Jokes (with Jim Ertner)
Sleeping Dogs Don't Lay (with Richard Dowis)
Super Funny Animal Jokes (with Jim Ertner)
Theme and Paragraph (with Philip Burnham)
A Treasury for Cat Lovers
A Treasury for Dog Lovers
A Treasury of Halloween Humor
A Tribute to Teachers
Wild & Wacky Animal Jokes (with Jim Ertner)
The Word Circus
Word Wizard
The Write Way (with Richard Dowis)

A Treasury of
Christmas Humor

Richard Lederer

International Punster of the Year

Illustrated by Jim McLean

Waterside Productions

Printed in the United States of America

First Printing, 2020

ISBN-13: 978-1-949001-41-9 print edition
ISBN-13: 978-1-949001-42-6 ebook edition

Waterside Productions
2055 Oxford Ave
Cardiff, CA 92007
www.waterside.com

to my friends in San Diego Mensa
and the memories of so many holiday parties
at the Lederer/van Egeren home

TABLE OF CONTENTS

THE STORY OF CHRISTMAS

Christmas is a major global holiday. For two mil-
lennia, people around the world have observed

Christmas with traditions both religious and secular. The Christmas story centers on the birth in Bethlehem of Jesus Christ, a spiritual leader who Christians believe is the son of God and whose teachings became the center of Christianity. Jesus's birth happened in a stable because there was no room at the inn for Joseph and Mary. To that stable journeyed three magi and shepherds with their flocks to join angels paying homage to the newborn child.

In the United States, the holiday is a joyous occasion illuminated by candles and graced by decorations, ornamented Christmas trees, poinsettias, traditional songs and carols, church services, family feasts, the exchange of gifts and greeting cards, the wait for Santa Claus to arrive, and the donning of ugly sweaters. December 25, Christmas Day, has been a federal holiday in America since 1870.

The Christmas traditions of trimming pine trees with ornaments, decking halls with boughs of holly, hanging mistletoe, and festooning homes with red, green, and silver decorations have become ingrained in Western culture. As with Chanukah, the Jewish festival of lights that occurs in the same season, human beings yearn for stories of light shining down on them during the dead of winter, the darkest time of the year. That's when people look for hope that brightness and warmth will return and life will go on.

A Stockingful of Christmas Riddles

How do sheep greet each other at Christmas?

"Season's Bleatings and Fleece Navidad!
Fleece on earth, good wool to sheep!"

And what did one sheep say to another sheep?

Every time I say, "Baa," you don't have to say,
"Humbug!"

Punnery is the trick of compacting two or more ideas within a single word or expression. It surprises us by flouting the law of nature that pretends that two things cannot occupy the same space at the same time. Punnery is an exercise of the mind in being concise. It challenges us to apply the greatest pressure per square syllable of language.

Punnery is a rewording experience, especially around Christmas. That's the time of year when people exchange hellos and good buys with each other and when mothers have to separate the men from the toys.

Where does Christmas come before Thanksgiving?
In the dictionary.

If athletes get athlete's foot, what do astronauts get?
Missile toe.

What do you call a Christmas bird dog?
A point setter.

Who is never hungry at Christmas?
The turkey. It's always stuffed.

Why is a Christmas turkey a fashionable bird?
Because he always appears well dressed for dinner.

What international disasters could happen if you dropped the Christmas turkey?
The downfall of Turkey, the breakup of China, and the overthrow of Greece.

What do you call a purveyor of turkey filling?
A stuffing stocker.

What's the best thing to put into a Christmas cake?
Your teeth.

What do you call an elephant at Christmas?
A noelephant.

What do you call parents standing in line to buy their daughters a popular doll?
A Barbie queue.

What do you call it when on the night before Christmas, children sneak halfway down the stairs to watch their parents putting gifts under the tree?

Christmas evesdropping.

What goes ho, ho, ho, whoosh, ho, ho, ho, whoosh?

Santa Claus caught in a revolving door.

What has a hundred legs and shouts, "Ho, ho, ho"?

A Santapede.

What do you call someone who doesn't believe in Santa?

A rebel without a Claus.

What's the difference between a knight and Santa's reindeer?

> *One slays the dragon. The other drags the sleigh on.*

What do movie stars burn in their fireplaces at Christmas time?

> *Holly wood.*

What do you call a chicken in the North Pole?

> *Lost.*

Why are Christmas trees like clumsy knitters?
They both drop their needles.

What's a gorilla's favorite Christmas song?
"Jungle Bells."

What's the favorite Christmas carol in the Arabian Desert?
"O Camel Ye Faithful."

Which of Santa's reindeer has the worst manners?
Rude-olph.

What did the peanut butter say to the grape on Christmas?
"'Tis the season to be jelly."

How did the classical musician remember the presents she wanted to buy for the holiday?

She kept a Christmas Chopin Liszt.

What is a little monster's favorite Christmas song?

"Eyesore Mummy Hissing Santa's Claws."

Who hides in the bakery at Christmas?

A mince spy.

If Christmas and Chanukah were combined, what song would be sung?

"Oy Vay, Maria."

Did you hear about the dyslexic devil worshipper?

He sold his soul to Santa.

What do you call a ghost hanging around Santa's Workshop?

A North Pole-tergeist.

What did the girl say when she was invited to portray the Virgin in a Christmas pageant?

"Oh, good. Now I can eat, drink, and be Mary."

What do you call a snowman in summer?

A puddle.

What do you get when you cross Santa Claus with a vagabond?

A ho, ho, hobo.

What do you get when you cross a snowman with a witch?

A cold spell.

What do you get when you cross a snowman with a vampire?

Frostbite.

What do you get when you cross a snowman with a bat?

Cold and flew symptoms.

What do you get when you cross a turkey with an octopus?

Enough drumsticks for a really big dinner.

What do you get when you cross a gift-wrapper with a criminal?

Ribbon Hood.

What do you get when you cross a Christmas tree with an iPad?

A pine Apple.

DON'T KNOCK
KNOCK-KNOCK JOKES

Knock, knock.
Who's there?
Wooden shoe.
Wooden shoe who?
Wooden shoe like to hear a bunch of Christmas knock-knock jokes?

Knock, knock.
Who's there?
Hearsay.
Hearsay who?
Hearsay parade of Christmas knock-knock jokes.

Knock, knock.
Who's there?
Yule.
Yule who?
Yule love these knock-knock jokes.

Knock, knock.
Who's there?
Hair comb.
Hair comb who?
Hair comb a bunch of knock-knock jokes.

Knock, knock.
Who's there?
Eyesore.
Eyesore who?
Eyesore hope you like knock-knock jokes.

Knock, knock.
Who's there?
Santa.
Santa who?
Santa letter to the North Pole.

Knock, knock.
Who's there?
Honda.
Honda who?
*Honda second day of Christmas my true love sent
to me two turtledoves…*

Knock, knock.
Who's there?
Hannah.
Hannah who?
Hannah partridge in a pear tree.

Knock, knock.
Who's there?
Donut.
Donut who?
Donut open till Christmas morning.

Knock, knock.
Who's there?
Dexter.
Dexter who?
Dexter halls with boughs of holly.

Knock, knock.
Who's there?
Avery Mary and Abby
Avery Mary and Abby who?
Avery Mary Christmas and an Abby New Year!

Knock, knock.
Who's there?
Irish.
Irish who?
Irish you a Merry Christmas!

Knock, knock.
Who's there?
Amsterdam.
Amsterdam who?
Amsterdam tired of these knock-knock jokes!

Knock, knock.
Who's there?
Consumption.
Consumption who?
Consumption be done to stop these ridiculous knock-knock jokes?

Knock, knock.
Who's there?
Celeste.
Celeste who?
Celeste time I tell you to knock it off!

Knock, knock.
Who's there?
Orange juice.
Orange juice who?
Orange juice glad that this'll be my very last knock-knock joke!

A PUNDERFUL
CHRISTMAS GAME

What's the difference between a one-wingéd angel and a two-wingéd angel?

It's a matter of a pinion.

It's my opinion that Yule love the game you're about to play. In each sentence below, fill in the blank or blanks with an expression commonly used at Christmastide or with an outrageous holiday pun. Answers repose at the end of this chapter.

1. On December 24, Adam's wife is known as _____ _____.

2. In Charles Dickens's *A Christmas Carol*, Scrooge was visited by the ghost of _____ _____.

3. An opinion survey in Alaska is called a _____ _____.

4. What word do Christmas angels use to greet each other? "_____."

5. What Christmas message is conveyed by these letters?

ABCDEFGHIJKMNOPQRSTUVWXYZ,
ABCDEFGHIJKMNOPQRSTUVWXYZ.

_____, _____

6. When the salt and the pepper say "Hi!" to each other, they're passing on _____ _____.

7. A holy man bereft of change could be called Saint _____.

8. When you cross a sheep with a cicada, you get a _____! _____!

9. A cat walking on the desert is bound to get _____ _____.

10. A quiet medieval armor-wearer is a _____ _____.

11. People who tell jokes on December 25 might be called _____ _____.

12. If you get Francis angry, you will _____.

13. On December 25, entertainers Burnett, Channing, and King are known as _____ _____.

14. Who's the most famous Christmas actress? Holly _____.

15. What do you call it when your Christmas tree explodes? O Tannen _____

Answers

1. Christmas Eve 2. Christmas Present 3. North poll
4. "Halo." 5. Noel, Noel (no *l*, no *l*)
6. seasons' greetings. 7. Nickeless. 8. Baa! Humbug!
9. sandy claws 10. silent knight
11. Christmas cards 12. frankincense 13. Christmas Carols 14. (Halle) Berry 15. bomb

THE ABDOMINAL SNOWMAN

In his biography *The Deer Sleigher,* James Fenimore Cooper wrote about the life of Santa Claus, also known as Saint Nicholas, Kriss Kringle, Father Christmas, or simply Santa. On the inside cover appears a photograph of Santa taken with Cooper's North Polaroid camera.

Did you know that Santa's first language is North Polish? He lovingly tends his garden, all the while laughing, "Hoe, hoe, hoe!"

Santa always wears the same suit, but it stays clean because Mrs. Claus washes it in Yule Tide. Part of that suit is a black belt, which Santa earned in karate. But no matter how much he works out, Saint Nick suffers from a number of health problems, including mistletoe, tinselitis, and hollytosis.

You'll also discover that Santa is the main Claus. His wife is a relative Claus. His children are dependent Clauses. As a group, they're all renoun Clauses. And the father of Father Christmas is, of course, a Grandfather Claus.

Santa's elves are subordinate Clauses. They're generous souls, not elfish. They study the elf-abet so that they can file correctly, but like all staff, they do all the work, and the fat guy in the suit gets all the credit.

As they make toys, the elves sing, "Love Me Tender." That's why they're known as Santa's little Elvis. And that's why, as they put the toys in boxes and prepare them for Santa's sack, they listen to wrap music. They also take a lot of elfies.

On Christmas Eve, Santa eats a jolly roll and leaps into his sleigh. Santa's sleigh always comes out first because it starts in the Pole position. It also gets terrific mileage because it has long-distance runners on each side.

Santa especially loves all his reindeer because every buck is deer to him. He puts bells on all his reindeer because their horns don't work. On the way to delivering gifts, he lets his coursers stop at the Deery Queen. Dasher and Dancer love washing their meals down with coffee because they are Santa's star bucks. Santa's own favorite food is Crisp Pringles.

Santa has the right idea: Deliver your products free because they're on the house. The fact that Santa works just one day a year is an inspiration to workers everywhere, but also explains why he gets paid only with cookies and milk.

When traveling in the sleigh in inclement weather, Santa gets icicles in his beard — real chin chillas, those! He sometimes removes all the bells from his sleigh and travels silently through the night. One day, he hopes to win a No Bell prize.

Santa is so Santa-mental that he confers gifts even on ghost children, who sing to Santa, "We'll Have a Boo Christmas Without You." Santa even delivers gifts to good little sharks while they sleep. They call him Santa Jaws.

Santa often guides his sleigh to Cape Canaveral. We know this because A SANTA AT NASA is a palindrome, a statement that reads the same forward and backward. When Santa Claus laughs while walking backward, what comes out is "oh, oh, oh!"

What's red and white and black all over? Santa Claus entering a home through a chimney. He loves sliding down chimneys because it soots him. But he actually has a fear of getting stuck. That fear is called Santa Claus-trophobia. The way to get him out of the chimney is to pour Santa Flush on him. When Santa falls down a chimney, he becomes Santa Klutz. Since Santa has to go up and down a wide variety of chimneys on Christmas, he gets a yearly flue shot.

Whatever the obstacles, Santa always delivers his presents in the Saint Nick of time. Then on December 25, Santa is a beat Nick.

There are five stages of a man's life:
(1) He believes in Santa Claus.
(2) He doesn't believe in Santa Claus.
(3) He dresses up to look like Santa Claus.
(4) He looks like Santa Claus.
(5) He believes he's Santa Claus.

ALL I NEED TO KNOW
I LEARNED FROM SANTA

- It's as much fun to give as it is to receive.
- Make children happy.
- Make your presents known.
- Be joyful and reliable, and people will believe in you.

- It's better to be nice than naughty.
- You better not cry, better not pout.
- It's okay if Santa's kids see Mommy kissing Santa Claus.
- Real estate is cheap in the North Pole.
- Provide honest employment to others, including elves and reindeer.
- Treat your reindeer well and they will work hard for you.

- Honor diversity in your staff, like Rudolph's red nose, which led the way.
- Feel free to ask for what you want.
- Chubby is okay.
- Beards and moustaches are in.
- Bright red can make anyone look good.
- Wearing a wide, black belt will make you look slimmer.
- If you come to town only once a year, everyone will think you're very important.
- Be thankful for kindness, especially when people leave you cookies and milk.
- Organize your data by making lists and checking them twice.
- Laughing, "Ho, Ho, Ho!" will spread joy to the world.

A FROSTY TREAT

Now it's time to break the ice and chill out with another Christmas icon.

Frosty and his wife live in the Snow belt in an icicle built for two on the snow banks of Lake Snowbegone. Where they live, it's so cold that Starbucks serves coffee on a stick! It's so cold that people have to scrape the ice off their glasses! It's so cold that if Lady Liberty lived there, she would have to put her torch inside her robe! It's so cold that pickpockets have their hands in their own pockets! It's so cold that people jump inside their freezers to warm up! It's so cold that Grandpa's teeth are chattering — in the glass! It's so cold that people have to chisel their dogs off fire hydrants!

Mr. and Mrs. Frosty love to hop on their snowmobiles or b-icicles to go dancing at snow balls. They send social media messages on the winternet, and say to everybody, "Have an ice day!" because they know that snowman is an island. They never blow their cool, go brrrrserk, have a meltdown, give you the cold shoulder, or make you cool your heels and feel left out in the cold. They deposit the profits from their snow jobs and slush fund in their local snow bank.

They love to belt out songs like "Baby It's Cold Outside," "There's Snow Place Like Home for the Holidays," "There's Snow Business Like Show Business," and "Freezer Jolly Good Fellow!" They listen to rappers like LL Cool J, Ice-T, and Ice Cube. They go out to watch ice hockey and the Ice Follies. And they sit in the Z row to watch movies like *The Big Chill*, *Ice Age*, *Frozen*, and *The Blizzard of Oz*.

Their favorite holiday figure is the Nor'Easter Bunny. They enjoy reading the poetry of Robert Frost and the novels of C.P. Snow and Leo Tolstoy, who wrote *War and Frozen Peas*. They often travel to Iceland or Chile.

The family's favorite foods are Frosted Flakes, Ice Krispies, cold cuts, iceberrrgers with chilly sauce, baked Alaska, cold slaw with Cool Ranch dressing, cake with a lot of icing, and snow cones topped with Cool Whip. They wash down each meal with a slushy.

Snowmen, snowwomen, and snowkids live their lives with some disadvantages. They walk around with two black eyes and sticks for arms. They can smell only carrots and taste only coal. They would get cold feet, but they don't have any feet. Instead, from sitting on the snow for so long, they develop polaroids.

When the Frosty chilled-ren were babies, Frosty and his wife placed a snowmobile over their crib. The kids call their parents Momsicle and Popsicle, and the parents advise the kids to put on their ice caps and snowshoes so they won't catch cold. If one of the chilled-ren get sick, mom and dad make sure that they take a chill pill.

Ho! Ho! Ho!
Christmas Quotes

- Mail your packages early so the post office can lose them in time for Christmas. – *Johnny Carson*
- I have all these people to give Christmas gifts to, and you know what I found? There are some very nice things at the 99-cent store. – *Ellen Degeneres*
- You know you're getting old when Santa starts looking younger. – *Robert Paul*
- Once again, we come to the holiday season, a deeply religious time that each of us observes, in his own way, by going to the mall of his choice. – *Dave Barry*
- I never believed in Santa Claus because I knew no white dude would ever come into my neighborhood after dark. – *Dick Gregory*

- I stopped believing in Santa Claus when I was six. Mother took me to see him in a department store, and he asked for my autograph. – *Shirley Temple*
- Let's be naughty and save Santa the trip. – *Gary Allan*
- Last Christmas I got no respect. In my stocking I got an Odor-Eater. – *Rodney Dangerfield*
- Christmas: It's the only religious holiday that's also a federal holiday. That way, Christians can go to their services, and everyone else can sit at home and reflect on the true meaning of the separation of church and state. – *Samantha Bee*
- A Christmas tree — the perfect gift for a guy. The plant is already dead. – *Jay Leno*
- Halloween is the beginning of the holiday shopping season. That's for women. The beginning of the holiday shopping season for men is Christmas Eve. – *David Letterman*

- What I don't like about office Christmas parties is looking for a job the next day. – *Phyllis Diller*
- On the thirteenth day of Christmas, my true love said to me, "I think I might be a hoarder." – *Jen Statsky*

- You can tell a lot about a person by the way they handle three things: a rainy day, lost luggage, and tangled Christmas tree lights. – *Maya Angelou*
- To avoid taking down my Christmas lights, I'm turning my house into an Italian restaurant. – *Patrick McLellan*

- Christmas: the only time of year when you sit in front of a dead tree eating candy out of a sock. – *Anonymous*
- What if it had been three Wise Women instead of three Wise Men? They would have asked directions, arrived on time, helped deliver the baby, cleaned the stable, made a casserole, brought practical gifts, and there would be Peace on Earth. – *Dandi Dailey Mackall*
- One Christmas I got a battery with a note saying, "Toy not included." – *Bernard Manning*
- All that time spent selecting and decorating, and a week after Christmas, you see the tree by the side of the road, like a mob hit. A car slows down, a door opens, and a tree rolls out. – *Jerry Seinfeld*

THE TRUE MEANINGS
OF CHRISTMAS

The great English etymologist Owen Barfield once wrote, "Words may be made to disgorge the past that is bottled up inside of them, as coal and wine, when we kindle or drink them, yield up their bottled sunshine." When we uncap the sunshine that is stored inside the many words that relate to the Christmas season, we discover that the light that streams forth illuminates centuries of human history and customs.

The word *Christmas* derives from the Old English *Cristes Maesse,* meaning "the festival mass of Christ." *Christmas* is a fine example of a disguised compound, a word formed from two independent morphemes (meaning-bearing elements) that have become so closely welded together that their individual identities have been lost.

Turns out that the word *holiday* is another disguised compound, descending from the Old English *haligdaeg,* "holy day." With the change in pronunciation has come a change in meaning so that holidays, such as Independence Day and Labor Day, are not necessarily holy. The *day* in *holiday* has also been transmuted so that an American can enjoy a three-day holiday.

The name *Christ* is a translation of the Hebrew word *messiah,* "the anointed one," rendered through the Greek as Christós. *Jesus* also reaches back to the ancient Hebrew name Yeshua, one of the names for God.

We learn about Jesus through the *gospels. Gospel* is yet another disguised compound, from the Old English *god,* "good," and *spel,* "news." The gospels of Matthew, Mark, Luke, and John spread the good news of the life and work of Christ. No surprise then that the four men who wrote the gospels are called *evangelists,* from the Greek *euaggelion,* which also means "good news."

The babe was born in *Bethlehem,* a Hebrew word meaning "house of bread." The Christ child was laid in a *manger,* a word related to the French verb *manger,* "to eat." Why? Because Jesus's crib was a large wooden box that usually served as a trough for feeding cattle.

We call the worship of the newborn babe the *Adoration,* from the Latin *adoratio*: *ad* – "to," and *oro* – "pray"; hence, "to pray to." Among those who came to worship were wise men from the East, *magi,* a Latin word for "magician" or "astrologer." The number of wise men is never mentioned in the gospels; we infer three from the gifts bestowed on the Christ child.

43

The Greek letter *chi*, spelled with an *X*, is the first letter of the word *Xristos*, which is Greek for Christ. *Xmas*, then, is actually a Greek derivative that does not eradicate the name of Christ from *Christmas*. The name of the holiday has been abbreviated as *Xmas* for five hundred years. Slogans like "Put the Christ back in Christmas" were coined by people who don't know the history of *X*. No offense intended then or now by the *X*.

Yuletide as a synonym for the Christmas season dates back to a pagan and then Christian period of feasting about the time of the winter solstice, December 22. The origin of *yule* is uncertain. One suggestion is that *yule* comes from the Gothic *giul* or *hiul*, which meant "wheel." In this context, *yule* signifies that the sun, like a wheel, has completed its annual journey. Whence the *tide* in *Yuletide*? From an Old English word meaning "time," as in *Eastertide*.

Christmas occurs shortly after the winter solstice, when the sun reaches its most southerly excursion relative to the celestial equator. The winter solstice enfolds the longest night of the year, just before the days slowly fill back up with brightness.

At the time of the summer and winter solstices, the sun, before journeying back toward the equator, appears to stand still. This phenomenon is reflected in the Latin roots of the word: *sol,* meaning "sun," and *sistere,* "to stand still."

Among the most fascinating Christmas etymologies are those for *Santa Claus* and *Kriss Kringle*. When the Dutch came to the New World during the seventeenth century, the figure of Saint Nikolaas, their patron saint, was on the first ship. After the Dutch lost control of New Amsterdam, *Sinterklaas* (a form of *Saint Nikolaas*) became anglicized into *Santa Claus.*

Kriss Kringle reflects an even more drastic change from one language to another. Immigrants from the Holy Roman Empire (now Germany, Austria, and Switzerland) settled in Pennsylvania in the seventeenth and eighteenth centuries. They held the custom that the Christ Child, "the Christ-kinkle," brought gifts for the children on Christmas Eve. When English-speaking settlers moved near these Pennsylvania Dutch (also known as Pennsylvania Deutsch), the Christ-kinkle became *Kriss Kringle*. By the 1840s, Kriss Kringle had irretrievably taken on the identity of St. Nicholas, or Santa Claus.

The word *carol* comes from the Greek word *choraulein*, "to accompany a chorus on a reed instrument." The word transmogrified to *carol* and came to signify a round dance. People originally performed carols on several occasions during the year. By the 1600s, carols involved singing only, and Christmas had become the main holiday for these songs.

Of the various plants associated with the Christmas season, the poinsettia possesses the most intriguing history etymologically. A Mexican legend tells of a penniless boy who presented to the Christ Child a beautiful plant with scarlet leaves that resembled the Star of Bethlehem. The Mexicans named the plant *Flor de la Noche Buena,* "Christmas Eve Flower." Dr. Joel Roberts Poinsett, the first U.S. minister to Mexico, came upon the red and green Christmas plant there in 1828 and brought it to the United States, where it was named in his honor in 1836. The poinsettia has become one of the most popular of Christmas plants — and one of the most misspelled words *(pointsettia, pointsetta, poinsetta)* in the English language.

Another botanical Christmas item is the pear tree. In the seasonal song "The Twelve Days of Christmas," have you ever wondered why the true love sends not only a partridge but also an entire pear tree? That's because in the early French version of the song the suitor gave only a partridge, which in French is rendered as *une pertriz*. A 1718 English version combined the two — "a partridge, une pertriz" — which, slightly corrupted, came out sounding like "a partridge in a pear tree." Ever since, the partridge has remained proudly perched in a pear tree.

A Merry Christ Mass and Happy Holy Days to all!

A Child's View of
Christmas

A mother was pleased with the Christmas card her son had made her but was puzzled about the scraggly-looking tree he had drawn. At the very top perched something that looked strangely like a bullet. Mom asked the boy if he would explain the drawing and tell why the tree itself was so bedraggled, instead of a fat pine tree. "It's not a Christmas tree," he said. "It's a cartridge in a bare tree."

❧ ❧ ❧

"And what would you like for Christmas?" asked a department store Santa Claus. The child stared at him open-mouthed, then gasped, "Didn't you get my e-mail?"

❧ ❧ ❧

A girl wrote in a Christmas card to her aunt, "I want to thank you for all the presents you have sent in the past, as well as all the ones you are going to send me this Christmas."

❧ ❧ ❧

Two daughters had been given parts in a Christmas pageant at their church. At dinner that night, they got into an argument as to who had the more important role. Finally, the ten-year-old said to her younger sister, "Well, you just ask Mom. She'll tell you it's much harder to be a virgin than it is to be an angel."

❖ ❖ ❖

A Sunday-school teacher was talking about the Christmas story and asked, "And what was the name of Jesus's mother?"

"Mary," all said.

"Now what his father's name?"

One little fellow raised his hand. "Virge."

"Virge? Where did you get that idea?"

"Well," answered the boy, "they always talk about the Virge 'n' Mary!"

❖ ❖ ❖

Another Sunday-school teacher asked her class, "What gifts did the three wise men give to the Christ child?"

"Gold!" answered one pupil.

"Frankincense," called out a second.

And a third volunteered, "Gift cards!"

❖ ❖ ❖

A youngster drew a Christmas scene that showed Santa with his sleigh and reindeer. There were the regular eight and Rudolph plus a strange looking tenth animal. The addition looked like a cross between a reindeer and a cow with a green nose. The youngster explained that it was Olive, the udder reindeer.

❧ ❧ ❧

Another Sunday-school teacher had the little ones draw pictures of the Bible stories. Little Emma proudly presented the teacher a picture of the journey to Bethlehem. The drawing showed an airplane flying over the desert. In the passenger area sat Joseph, Mary, and little Jesus.

"The drawing is fine," said the teacher, "but who's that way up front?"

Answered the girl, "That's Pontius the Pilot."

❧ ❧ ❧

When yet another Sunday-school teacher asked her student why there was a dog in the nativity drawing, the fledgling artist explained that it was a German shepherd. That shepherd has been joined in the gallery of Sunday-school portraiture by a grinning ursine with crossed eyes — Gladly, the Cross-Eyed Bear, of course.

⚜ ⚜ ⚜

Sunday-school boys and girls not only produce graphic misinterpretations of the Bible in their drawings, they also rewrite biblical history with amazing grace. It is astonishing what happens to the Christmas story when young scholars around the world retell it:

The King James Virgin of the Bible tells us that when Mary heard that she was the Mother of Jesus, she sang the Magna Carta and wrapped him in toddler clothes. Jesus was born because Mary had an immaculate contraption.

In the Gospel of Luke they named him Enamel. St. John, the Blacksmith, dumped water on his head. Joseph and Mary took Jesus with them to Jerusalem because they couldn't get a babysitter. When the three wise guys from the East Side arrived, they found Jesus laid in the manager. When Jesus grew up, he explained the Golden Rule: "Do one to others before they do one unto you."

A Cat's Twelve Days
of Christmas

Have you ever noticed that, by the end of "The Twelve Days of Christmas," the house of the woman who tells the story would be crammed with an aviary of one-hundred-and-forty-two assorted birds and a hundred-and-forty hyperactive humans?

Here's a far simpler version:

> On the twelfth day of Christmas, my
> human gave to me
> Twelve bags of catnip,
> Eleven cans of tuna,
> Ten ornaments hanging,
> Nine wads of Kleenex,

Eight pillow beds,
Seven litter boxes,
Six rising ramps,
Five scratching posts,
Four cat climbers,
Three cutesy toys,
Two fuzzy mice,
And a hamster in a plastic ball!

REINVENTING CHRISTMAS

In 1822, the Reverend Clement Clarke Moore, a literature professor at a theological seminary in New York City, wrote for his children what many believe is the best-known poem in the English language, "A Visit from Saint Nicholas."

Usually titled "The Night Before Christmas" Moore's verses powerfully influenced the iconography of Santa Claus — his plump and jolly white-bearded look, his means of transportation, the names of his reindeer, and the tradition of his delivering toys to boys and girls on Christmas Eve. On that night before Christmas, many parents read this poem to their children.

You can read Moore's poem in the chapter coming up.

Later in the nineteenth century, another New Yorker, Thomas Nast, enlarged the image of Santa Claus with his artist's pen and brush. Known as the Father of the American Cartoon, Nast remembered that when he was a little boy in southern Germany, every Christmas a fat old man gave toys and cakes to children. So, when he sketched and painted Santa, his portraits looked like the kindly old man of his childhood.

Santa Claus had been represented in various ways, but Nast, influenced by the "right jolly old elf" depicted in Moore's poem, created the figure we know today. Over the course of thirty years of drawing for *Harper's Weekly* magazine, he baked into our culture his image of Santa Claus — his jolly girth, his white beard and moustache, his bright red-and-white-trimmed coat, trousers, and hat, his black belt and boots, and his sack of toys. He also drew Mrs. Claus and set the Clauses' workshop at the North Pole.

Across the sea in England, Charles Dickens was born into an impoverished family. His father served a term in debtors' prison, and Charles worked as a child laborer in a London boot-blacking factory. From such unpromising origins, he rose to become the best-selling writer of his time and one of the most enduring and quotable writers of all time. The rags-to-riches life of Charles Dickens became more fantastic than any of his stories.

In 1843, within the brief compass of six weeks, Dickens gave the world *A Christmas Carol*. The influence of that Christmas present is towering. The story's glowing message — the importance of charity and good will toward all humankind — struck a resonant chord in England and the United States and deepened the celebration of the holiday. Although Christmases in eastern England were rarely snowy,

Dickens's backdrop of a blizzardy London in his *Carol* stuck with readers and helped create our expectations of a "White Christmas."

Today, we're likely to call anyone who is not in the Christmas spirit a Scrooge and give them a sarcastic "Bah! Humbug!" Most of us know that we owe this phrase to Charles Dickens, but hardly anyone realizes that he also popularized the greeting "Merry Christmas." Ebenezer Scrooge's visiting nephew greets his uncle with it in the very first chapter. In all his curmudgeonly glory, Scrooge fires back, "'Merry Christmas!' What right have you to be merry? Every idiot who goes about with 'Merry Christmas' on his lips should be boiled with his own pudding and buried with a stake of holly through his heart!" After that episode, "Merry Christmas" lodged in readers' minds and hearts.

Without Charles Dickens's slim stack of messy manuscript pages that came to be known as *A Christmas Carol*, Christmas today might still be a relatively minor holiday with no carolers and no large family gatherings for turkey dinners.

THE NIGHT BEFORE CHRISTMAS

'Twas the night before Christmas,
When all through the house,
Not a creature was stirring,
Not even a mouse.

The stockings were hung
By the chimney with care,
In hopes that St. Nicholas
Soon would be there.

The children were nestled
All snug in their beds,
While visions of sugarplums
Danced in their heads.

And mamma in her kerchief
And I in my cap
Had just settled down
For a long winter's nap,

When out on the lawn
There arose such a clatter,
I sprang from my bed
To see what was the matter.

Away to the window
I flew like a flash,
Tore open the shutters
And threw up the sash.

The moon on the breast
Of the new-fallen snow
Gave a luster of midday
To objects below.

When what to my wondering
Eyes did appear,
But a miniature sleigh
And eight tiny reindeer.

With a little old driver,
So lively and quick,
I knew in a moment
He must be St. Nick.

More rapid than eagles
His coursers they came,
And he whistled and shouted
And called them by name:

"Now Dasher! Now Dancer!
Now Prancer and Vixen!
On Comet! On Cupid!
On Donner and Blitzen!

To the top of the porch!
To the top of the wall!
Now dash away, dash away,
Dash away all!"

As leaves that before
The wild hurricane fly,
When they meet with an obstacle,
Mount to the sky.

So up to the housetop
The coursers they flew
With the sleigh full of toys,
And St. Nicholas, too —

And then, in a twinkling,
I heard on the roof
The prancing and pawing
Of each little hoof.

As I drew in my head
And was turning around,
Down the chimney St. Nicholas
Came with a bound.

He was dressed all in fur,
From his head to his foot,
And his clothes were all tarnished
With ashes and soot.

A bundle of toys
He had flung on his back,
And he looked like a peddler
Just opening his pack.

His eyes, how they twinkled!
His dimples, how merry!
His cheeks were like roses,
His nose like a cherry!

His droll little mouth
Was drawn up like a bow,
And the beard on his chin
Was as white as the snow.

The stump of a pipe
He held tight in his teeth,
And the smoke, it encircled
His head like a wreath.

He had a broad face
And a little round belly
That shook when he laughed,
Like a bowl full of jelly.

He was chubby and plump,
A right jolly old elf,
And I laughed when I saw him,
In spite of myself.

A wink of his eye
And a twist of his head
Soon gave me to know
I had nothing to dread.

He spoke not a word,
But went straight to his work
And filled all the stockings,
Then turned with a jerk,

And, laying his finger
Aside of his nose
And giving a nod,
Up the chimney he rose.

He sprang to his sleigh,
To his team gave a whistle,
And away they all flew
Like the down of a thistle.

But I heard him exclaim,
Ere he drove out of sight,
"Happy Christmas to all,
And to all a good night!"

A Dog's Night
Before Christmas

Inspired by Clement Clark Moore's enduring poem and some internet parodies, I present my doggy version, of "The Night Before Christmas":

'Twas the night before Christmas,
When all through the house,
Not a creature was stirring,
Not even a mouse.

The stockings were hung
By the chimney with care,
In hopes that St. Nicholas
Soon would be there.

My dogs, they were nestled
All snug in their beds,
While visions of chewy toys
Danced in their heads.

When up on the roof
There arose such a clatter.
I sprang from my bed
To see what was the matter.

And what to my wondering
Eyes should appear
But a toy-laden sleigh
With eight mighty reindeer.

With a jolly old driver
So lively and quick.
I knew in a moment
It must be Saint Nick.

With a flutter of ashes
And flurry of soot,
He slid down the chimney
With all of his loot.

My precious dogs stood there,
So regal and proud,
Guarding our home
With their barks oh so loud.

Santa Paws showed no fear,
And he called them by name.
He knew in his heart
They were gentle and tame.

He brought out his list,
Began checking it twice.
"My beauties, I see
That all year you've been nice.

"I have in my bag
Many toys, and much more.
Please tell me, you puppies,
What you're longing for."

My dogs talked to each other,
Much to my surprise,
And then turned to Santa
With tears in their eyes.

"We have chewies and balls
And ropes to be tugged.
We are pampered and coddled
And petted and hugged.

"But for Christmas, dear Santa,
We have but one care:
That all dogs be loved
Just as much as we are.

"We want no dog beaten,
No dog starved or chained.
We want no dog abused
Or abandoned or maimed.

"We want that all dogs,
No matter what size,
See true love reflected
In their masters' eyes."

Then Santa Paws paused
To gather his wits.
"I cannot stop humans
From being such twits.

"Each dog's so devoted
And is such a treasure
They just want to be loved
And to give humans pleasure.

"This is a bright lesson
That I'll try to teach,
And maybe your wish
Will be within my reach."

Santa Paws then turned to me,
His face wet with tears:
"Be proud of your puppies.
They all are such dears."

He planted a kiss
On each beautiful head:
"Now you gentle giants
Go right off to bed.

"Think only good thoughts,
And dream only good dreams.
Of running and playing
And jumping in streams."

And then Santa Paws
Disappeared in a poof,
And I heard him laugh loudly
Up there on the roof.

He jumped in his sleigh,
To his team gave a whistle.
And off he then flew,
Like the down on a thistle.

And I heard him exclaim
Ere he drove out of sight,
"Yappy Howl-a-days to all,
And to dogs a good life!"

AND TO ALL
A GOOD LAUGH

'Twas the night after Christmas,
And all through the house,
Not a garment would fit me,
Not even a blouse.

'Twas the night after Christmas,
And all round my hips
Were Fannie May candies
That sneaked past my lips.

I stored chocolate fudge
In the freezer with care,
In hopes that my thighs
Would forget it was there.

The cookies, the eggnog —
All I love to taste —
At the holiday parties
They all went to waist.

Then out in the pantry
Arose such a clatter.
I sprang from my bed
To see what was the matter.

When I got on the scales,
There arose such a number
That I scarcely could walk.
It was more like a lumber.

I remembered the marvelous
Meals I'd prepare —
The beef, gravies, sauces,
And pies everywhere,

The wine and the rum balls,
The bread and the cheese,
And the fact that I never
Said, "No, thank you, please."

The sweet-coated Santa,
Those sugared reindeer —
I closed my eyes tightly,
But still I could hear,

"On Jenny Craig, Stillman,
On Atkins, on TOPS" —
A Weight Watchers dropout
From sugar detox.

My droll little mouth
And my round little belly,
Which shook when I laughed
Like a bowl full of jelly.

Wearing Lane Bryant
From my head to my dress,
My clothes were all bulging
From rampant excess.

So away with the fruitcake,
The sour cream dips.
Get rid of the sugarplums,
Crackers, and chips.

Every last bit of food
That I crave must be banished
Till all the additional
Ounces have vanished.

Then I promise to cut
All my portions in half.
"Merry Christmas to all —
And to all a good laugh!"

A JUMBLED CHRISTMAS

Unscramble each set of letters to form a Christmas word. Examples: RATS = *star*, DOILYHA = *holiday*.

1. GLO
2. BLESL
3. LONE
4. SUJES
5. STRHIC
6. IMAG
7. FISGT
8. SOLCAR
9. OYST
10. ULYE
11. OWNS
12. GGGONE

13. DARCS
14. GERMAN
15. CHEERC
16. TANAS
17. LUCAS
18. GLEAN
19. SOPLEGS
20. GLEISH
21. LOYHL
22. OMLETSITE
23. DINERERE

24. SOFTRY
25. TRUEFICAK
26. SHAMEIS
27. MASTSIRCH
28. SILENT
29. GRINIV
30. PRESSHEHD
31. STONERMAN
32. ITASTEPINO
33. BRINGAGREED
34. THEHELMBE
35. AROADINTO

Answers

1. log 2. bells 3. noel 4. Jesus 5. Christ
6. magi 7. gifts 8. carols 9. toys 10. Yule
11. snow 12. eggnog 13. cards 14. manger 15. crèche

77

16. Santa 17. Claus 18. angel 19. gospels 20. sleigh
21. holly 22. mistletoe 23. reindeer 24. Frosty
25. fruitcake
26. Messiah 27. Christmas 28. tinsel 29. virgin
30. shepherds
31. ornaments 32. poinsettia 33. gingerbread
34. Bethlehem 35. adoration

A Pun-thology
of Christmas Songs

Children and other people are innocently brilliant at concocting original interpretations of the boundaries that separate words. For example, in the song "The Twelve Days of Christmas," "Ten lords a-leaping" becomes "Ten lawyers leaving." "Nine ladies dancing" becomes "Nine lazy Hansons." "Six geese a-laying" becomes "Six geezers laying." "On the first day of Christmas, my true love gave to me" becomes "On the first day of Christmas, my tulip gave to me," and "a partridge in a pear tree" becomes "a paltry tin-affair tree."

In "Santa Claus is Coming to Town," "He's makin' a list and checkin' it twice" changes into "He's makin' a list and chicken and rice." In "Winter Wonderland," "Later on, we'll conspire" transforms into "Later on, milk and spiders" and "Parson Brown" into "sparse and brown."

Try singing along with these takes on holiday favorites, revised by America's misspelt youth:

- Good King Wenceslas' car backed out
  On a piece of Stephen.
- Deck the halls with Buddy Holly.
- Noel, Noel. Barney's the king of Israel.
- Bells on bobtail ring,
  Making spareribs bright.
- You'll go down in Listerine.
- O, come froggy faithful.

- Chipmunks roasting on an open fire.
- Oh, what fun it is to ride
  In a one-horse, soap, and hay.
- What a friend we have in cheeses.
- Where shepherds washed
  Their socks by night.
- Get dressed, ye married gentlemen.
  Get huffing you this May.
- God and sinners dressed in style.
- Round John Virgin, mother and child,
  Holy Vincent, so tender and mild.

These charming examples are inadvertent. When the similarity between two words is crafted purposely, the result is a pun. A set-up pun is a conspiracy of narrative and word play. In set-up punnery, the punster contrives an imaginary situation that leads up to a climax punningly, cunningly, and stunningly based on a well-known expression or title. In a good set-up pun, we groan at the absurdity of the situation while admiring the ingenuity with which the tale reaches its foreordained conclusion.

Now it's time to be a groan-up while admiring the following stories as they lead up to the Christmas *pun*ch lines:

Rudolph, a dedicated Russian communist and important rocket scientist, was about to launch a large satellite. His wife, a fellow scientist at the base, urged Rudolph to postpone the launch because, she asserted, a hard rain was about to fall. Their collegial disagreement soon escalated into a furious argument that Rudolph closed by shouting, "Rudolph, the Red, knows rain, dear!"

❈ ❈ ❈

A woman went to her dentist because she felt something wrong in her mouth. The dentist looked inside and said, "That new upper plate I put in for you six months ago is eroding. What have you been eating?"

The woman replied, "All I can think of is that about four months ago I made some asparagus and put some delicious Hollandaise sauce on it. I loved it so much I now put it on everything — meat, toast, fish, vegetables, everything!"

"Well," said the dentist, "that's the problem. Hollandaise sauce is made with lots of lemon juice, which is highly corrosive. It's eaten away your upper plate. I'll make you a new plate, and this time I'll use chrome."

"Why chrome?" asked the patient.

"It's simple," replied the dentist. "Dental researchers have concluded that there's no plate like chrome for the Hollandaise!"

⚜ ⚜ ⚜

A group of chess-playing fanatics would gather each morning in a hotel lobby to brag about their greatest victories. It seemed that each player had only triumphs and awesome feats of skill to his credit. Then came a day when the hotel manager barred the group from the lobby because he couldn't stand to hear a bunch of chess nuts boasting in an open foyer.

⚜ ⚜ ⚜

Three circus midgets decided to change professions. They reviewed their options and decided to move to China and start a business together in that burgeoning economy. They bought a factory in Beijing and started manufacturing material to use in building highways for China's expanding transportation system. They shrewdly cornered the market on a black, sticky substance used to cover the roads they were building. They became known as the three wee kings of Orient tar.

❖ ❖ ❖

One of rock and roll's earliest and greatest performers was the incomparable Buddy Holly. Despite his bespectacled, nerdy appearance, the man really knew how to ignite an audience. But when his fans saw that Buddy had performed the closing song, they would fly into a collective rage because the concert was over. They would smash chairs, storm the stage, and tear down the curtain. As a result, no theater owner would hire Buddy. They feared that their patrons would wreck the hall with bows of Holly.

NAME THAT
CHRISTMAS CAROL

When I was a callow youth, my neighborhood buddies and I used to sing a learned lyric that played with levels of diction:

Propel, propel, propel your craft
Placidly down the liquid solution.
Ecstatically, ecstatically, ecstatically, ecstatically.
Existence is but a delusion.

Translated into clear and simple English, our polysyllabic poem turned out to be "Row, row, row your boat."

These days, my adolescent adventure in oblique obfuscation and inflated jargon has evolved into challenging game of sesquipedalian Christmas songs. Here are thirty pompously inflated titles of Christmas carols and songs that you hear and perhaps sing during the month of December. Your task is to translate each ponderous, puffed-up version back into its original form.

Examples: The Primary Yuletide = "The First Noel." The Diminutive Striped Squirrel Melody = "The Chipmunk Song." Answers repose at the end of this chapter.

1. O Miniature Nazarene Village 2. Antlered Quadruped with the Cerise Proboscis 3. Post-Dusk, Soundless and Sacred 4. O Locomote Hitherward, All You Steadfast 5. In a Distant Bovine Animal Feeding Station

6. While Vigilant Herdsmen Nocturnally Observed Their Pastoral Woollies 7. My Sole Desire for the Yuletide is Receipt of Twin Incisors 8. Celestial Messengers from Splendid Empires 9. The Event Transpired at the Darkest Time with Visibility Unlimited 10. Ornament the Corridors with Sprigs of Berry-Bearing Evergreen

11. Exuberation to This Terrestrial Sphere 12. Omnipotent Supreme Being Bestow Respite Upon

You Rollicking Chevaliers 13. The Diminutive Fledgling Male Percussionist 14. Roly-Poly Personification Fabricated of Compressed Mounds of Crystal Granules 15. Who is the Mysterious Pre-adolescent?

16. On December 25, I Hearkened to the Tintinnabulation. 17. Perambulating Through a December Solstice Fantasy Topography 18. I am Experiencing a Soporific Vision of an Alabaster Nativity Celebration 19. Tintinnabulation of Vacillating Pendules in Inverted Metallic Caps 20. I Perceived My Maternal Parent's Indiscretion with Kriss Kringle

21. Are You Detecting the Same Aural Sensations As I Am? 22. Listen! Celestial Cherubic Messengers Generate Harmonious Sounds 23. We, a Trio of Reigning Monarchs of the Far East, Exist 24. A Rotund, Hirsute Gift-Bearer Draws Nigh to Our Municipality 25. The Dozen Twenty-Four-Hour Intervals of Yuletide

26. Proceed Forth Declaiming upon a Geological Protuberance 27. Castanea Seeds Incandescing

in an Uncovered Conflagration 28. Cup-Shaped Instruments Fashioned of a Whitish Metallic Element 29. The Aquifoliaceae and the Hedera 30. I Perceived a Trio of Nautical Vessels

Answers

1. O Little Town of Bethlehem 2. Rudolph the Red Nose Reindeer 3. Silent Night, Holy Night 4. O Come, All Ye Faithful 5. Away in a Manger

6. While Shepherds Watched Their Flocks by Night 7. All I Want for Christmas is My Two Front Teeth 8. Angels from the Realms of Glory 9. It Came upon a Midnight Clear 10. Deck the Halls with Boughs of Holly

11. Joy to the World 12. God Rest Ye Merry, Gentlemen 13. The Little Drummer Boy 14. Frosty the Snowman 15. What Child Is This?

16. I Heard the Bells on Christmas Day 17. Walking Through a Winter Wonderland 18. I'm Dreaming of a White Christmas 19. Jingle Bells 20. I Saw Mommy Kissing Santa Claus

21. Do You Hear What I Hear? 22. Hark, the Herald Angels Sing 23. We Three Kings of Orient Are 24. Santa Claus is Coming to Town 25. The Twelve Days of Christmas

26. Go Tell It on the Mountain 27. Chestnuts Roasting On an Open Fire 28. Silver Bells 29. The Holly and the Ivy 30. I Saw Three Ships

Scoring

25-30
You have all the Yuletide spirit you need.

15-24
You could use a little something in your stocking.

0-14
Are you sure you have the right holiday?

HAPPY NEW YEAR!

The passing of one year into the beginning of another is marked around the world by New Year's Eve customs ranging from high-spirited parties to solemn prayer and thought. The biggest and most famous New Year's party takes place in New York City. Millions of people around the world watch the ginormous crystal ball drop over Times Square.

"Auld Lang Syne," written by the Scottish poet Robert Burns, is the song most identified with New Year's celebrations:

Should auld acquaintance be forgot,
    And never brought to mind?
Should auld acquaintance be forgot,
    And auld lang syne?

For auld lang syne, my dear,
    For auld lang syne,
We'll take a cup of kindness yet,
    For auld lang syne.

We all know "Auld Lang Syne," even though few of us really know what it means, which happens to be "old long since" or "long ago," appropriate to the time when we review the joys and disappointments of the past year and hope for the best to come. The song was first popularized in 1929 by Guy Lombardo and his Royal Canadians orchestra.

On January 1, we make New Year's resolutions, vowing to better ourselves in the coming year. Many of these resolutions are forgotten as soon as they're made, but the sentiment remains noble. In fact, eighty percent of all New Year's resolutions are broken by the end of February. I believe that taking a few moments to reflect on our shortcomings and optimistically plan to overcome them is better than making no attempt at all. And sometimes, when we are ready for change, those resolutions do stick — some for a lifetime.

On New Year's Eve, I'm in a hurry. I have only a few hours left to do all the things I've resolved not to do in the new year. When they drop the ball in Times Square, it's a reminder of what I did all last year. So for this year,

- I resolve not to drop the ball.
- I resolve to get better at pretending to know the words to "Auld Lang Syne."
- Three resolutions I can actually keep are I resolve not to diet all year long, to drink more beer, and to always leave the toilet seat up.

- I resolve to take all the Christmas lights down by Easter.
- I resolve to lose weight by inventing an anti-gravity machine.
- If that doesn't work, I resolve to help all my friends gain ten pounds so I look skinnier.
- I resolve to read more, so I'm going to put the captions up on my TV screen.
- I resolve to be more positive and less sarcastic. Yeah, sure.
- I resolve to stop putting my foot in my mouth, and I bet you resolve to lose weight. Right?
- I resolve to stop letting my mood swings control my life. Nah, I'm not up for that.
- I resolve to stop repeating myself again and again and again.
- I resolve to stop repeating myself again and again and again.
- I resolve to stop hanging out with people who ask me about my New Year's resolutions.
- I resolve to break my New Year's resolutions. That way I can succeed at something.

As your reader-friendly Attila the pun, my final Gnu Year's resolution is to tell ewe a gazelleon times how much I caribou ewe, deer. I'm a wildebeest of a punster, and you're thinking, "Unicorniest fellow I've ever met!" but I'm not out to buffalo or a llama ewe, so alpaca bag and hightail it out of here in camelflage.

❧ ❧ ❧

Christmas was over. Santa Claus and his reindeer finally had a chance to rest. They had done a good job, and they deserved it. Rudolph the Red-Nosed Reindeer had a chance to do something he had wanted to do for a long time. He made an appointment with a plastic surgeon because he was so sensitive about his looks. It wasn't his glowing red nose that he wanted changed. He was proud of that nose and the help he and it had given to Santa. No, he was sensitive about his long ears, which were much more prominent than the ears of the average reindeer, or rabbit for that matter.

So one week after Christmas, Rudolph's doctor performed the surgery, and since that time, on January 1, Rudolph goes around saying, "Happy New Ears Day!"

Here's how other animals say it:

from a puppy: "Yappy New Year!"
a duck: "Quacky New Year!"
a cat: "Happy Mew Year!"
a bovine: "Happy Moo Steer!"
a cat: "Happy Mew Year!"

a turtle: "Snappy New Year!"

a large water beast: "Hippo New Year!"
a skunk: "Happy Eeewww Year!"
an expectant antelope: "Happy Gnu Deer!"
a wolf: "Happy Arrrroooo Year!"
a kangaroo: "Hoppy New Year!"

Here are the ways people in various jobs wish you a great year:

a journalist: "Happy News Year!"
a hip hop artist: "Rappy New Year!"
a mechanic: "Happy Lube Gear!"
a job counselor: "Happy New Career!"

a bartender: "Happy New Beer!"
a maple syrup seller: "Sappy New Year!"
a programmer: "Appy New Year!"
a zoological director: "Happy Zoo Year!"
a detective: "Happy Clue Year!"

a cartographer: "Mappy New Year!"
a cobbler: "Happy Shoe Year!"
a Greek mythologist: "Harpy New Year!"
a sea captain: "Happy Crew Year!"
a lawyer: "Happy Sue Year!"
a priest: "Happy Pew Year!"
a surfer: "Happy Dude Year!"
a pirate: "Happy Blue Beard!"
a men's clothier: "Natty New Year!"

What's "New"?

To celebrate the new year, here are twenty brief definitions of words that contain the sound *noo* or *n(y)oo* in them. Sometimes the word will contain the actual letters *new*, as in *newspaper*. In other instances, the word will have a different spelling, as in *nuisance*.

Let's begin with words that start with the sound of the adjective *new*. From each definition, identify each word.

1. naked
2. had knowledge of
3. mental disorder
4. middle of the day
5. metaphor for the head
6. lung disease
7. nourishing
8. wildebeest
9. report of recent events
10. acute nerve pain
11. small salamander
12. masculine, feminine, and …
13. the necktie in a necktie party
14. shade of distinction

15. of marriage-
    able age.

16. relating to mat-
    ters atomic

17. elementary
    atomic particle

18. center of Three
    Musketeers

19. large Canadian island

20. scientist bopped
    by an apple

Answers

1. nude 2. knew 3. neurosis 4. noon 5. noodle
6. pneumonia 7. nutritious 8. gnu 9. news 10. neuralgia
11. newt 12. neuter 13. noose 14. nuance 15. nubile
16. nuclear 17. neutron 18. nougat 19. Newfoundland
20. Newton

As an additional challenge, here are twenty more words containing the sound *noo* or *nyoo*, but not at the beginning of the word:

1. refresh
2. yearly
3. hint
4. Eskimo people
   of Canada
5. famous choo-choo
6. Charlie Brown's dog
7. looking down
   one's nose
8. to sleep
9. tendon
10. food list
11. countless
12. having little substance
13. naïve young woman
14. broad street or road
15. keep on, persist
16. locale
17. income stream
18. entourage
19. light, narrow boat
20. by hand

Answers

1. renew 2. annual 3. insinuation, innuendo. 4. Inuit
5. Chattanooga
6. Snoopy 7. snooty 8. snooze 9. sinew 10. menu
11. innumerable 12. tenuous 13. ingénue 14. avenue
15. continue
16. venue 17. revenue 18. retinue 19. canoe 20. manual

LAST WORDS

Happy New Year! It's nice to have You Near!

In the coming year, may you try not only to hear, but to listen; not only to write, but to communicate; not only to talk, but to say something. May your thoughts and aspirations become words that serve to build bridges from mind to mind and from heart to heart, creating a fellowship of those who would hold fast to that which is good.

ACKNOWLEDGMENTS

I am grateful for permission to adapt in *A Treasury of Christmas Humor* versions of some items that have appeared in my Gibbs Smith and Marion Street Press books.

Author Biography

Richard Lederer is the author of more than fifty books about language, history, and humor, including his best-selling *Anguished English* series and his current books, *The Joy of Names* and *A Treasury of Halloween Humor.* He is a founding co-host of *A Way With Words,* broadcast on Public Radio.

Dr. Lederer's syndicated column, *Lederer on Language,* appears in newspapers and magazines throughout the United States. He has been named International Punster of the Year and Toastmasters International's Golden Gavel winner.

He lives in San Diego with his wife, Simone van Egeren.

richardhlederer@gmail.com / verbivore.com

PORTRAIT OF THE ARTIST

Jim McLean enjoyed a thirty-three year career as a professor of art. He has exhibited internationally and has works in a number of museums, universities, and private collections. Since his retirement in 1994, Jim's interest in cartooning led him to a productive collaboration with Richard Lederer, for whom he has illustrated fifteen books.

mcle231@bellsouth.net

Made in the USA
Columbia, SC
24 October 2021